CW00401698

SONGS OF LIGHT

Selections from the Psalms with prayer meditations

Photos by:	Page:
Ben Alex:	27.
Bavaria:	20-21, 52-53.
Bedding:	76-77.
Colorific:	6-7.
Siegfried Eigstler:	68-69.
Jan Flop:	33.
R.C. Hayes:	50-51, 74-75.
Mauritius:	cover photo, 5, 12-13, 24-25, 41, 64-65, 80.
Jean-Paul Nacivet:	72-73.
Stockphoto:	18-19, 26, 30-31, 40, 46-47, 58-59, 78-79.
Tony Stone:	8-9, 10-11, 14-15, 16, 17, 22-23, 28-29, 34-35, 36-37, 38-39, 44-45, 48-49, 54-55, 60-61, 62-63, 66-67, 70-71.
Alice Tarnanen:	42, 43.
Urpo Tarnanen:	32, 56-57.

Printed in Singapore by TWP.

ISBN 87 87732 89 0

Distribution in the United Kingdom:
Scandinavia Publishing House
Grafton Place
Worthing
Sussex
BN 111 QX
England
Tel. (0903) 209983/4

SONGS OF LIGHT

Selections from the Psalms with prayer meditations

Scripture text from The Holy Bible, New International Version

Text by Marlee Alex
Edited by Jørgen Vium Olesen

Scandinavia

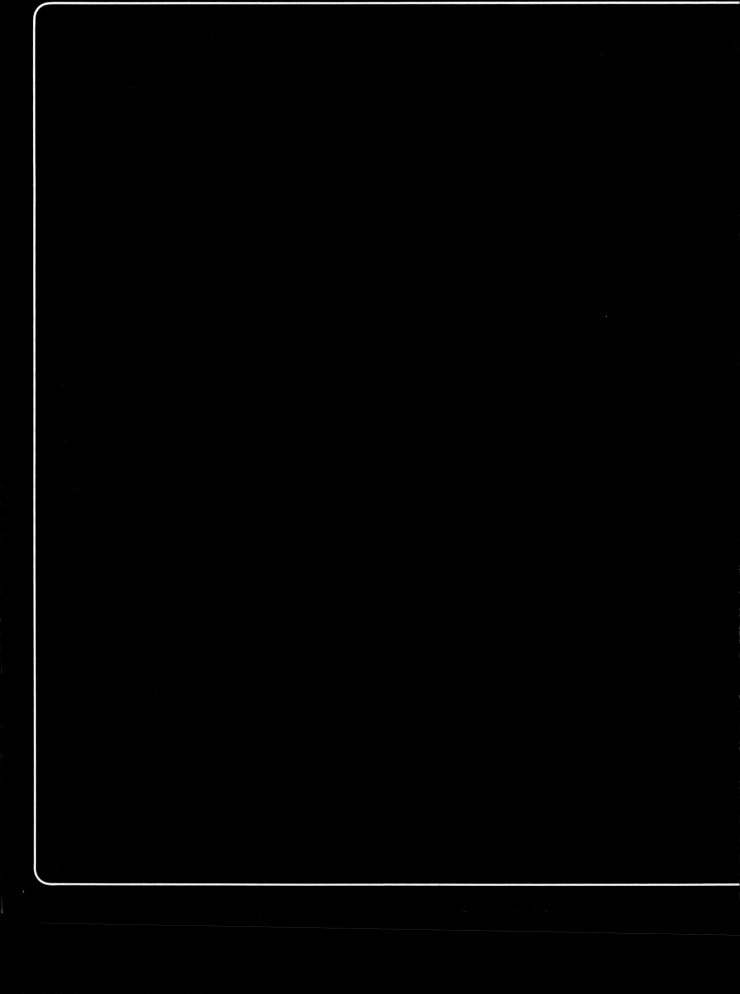

*Let the morning
bring me word of Your unfailing
love, for I have put my
trust in You.*

Blessed is he whose help
is the God of Jacob, whose hope is
in the Lord his God, the Maker of heaven
and earth, the sea, and everything
in them – the Lord, who remains
faithful forever.

Look to the Lord

I lift up my eyes to you, to you whose throne is in heaven.

I lift up my eyes to you, to you whose throne is in heaven.
As the eyes of slaves look to the hand of their master, as the
eyes of a maid look to the hand of her mistress, so our eyes
look to the Lord our God, till he shows us his mercy.

Have mercy on us, O Lord, have mercy on us, for we have
endured much contempt.
We have endured much ridicule from the proud, much
contempt from the arrogant.

*Have mercy with me Lord. I serve You
gladly, it's just the others who are so
difficult to submit to! They seem to take no
notice of how they humiliate me. They wear
away at my soul until I can't look them in
the eye. But I'll lift my eyes to You Father,
You who know me through and through. I'll
keep a steady gaze on You until I can find
grace to bear the others also.*

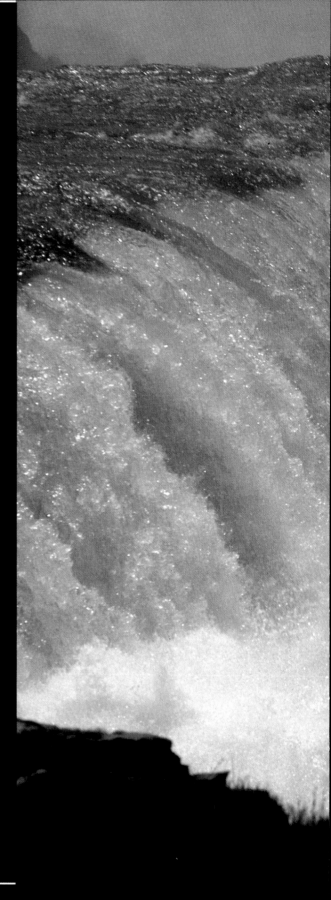

The Snare Has Been Broken

Praise be to the Lord, who has not let us be torn by their teeth. We have escaped like a bird out of the fowler's snare; the snare has been broken, and we have escaped.

If the Lord had not been on our side– let Israel say– if the Lord had not been on our side when men attacked us, when their anger flared against us, they would have swallowed us alive; the flood would have engulfed us, the torrent would have swept over us, the raging waters would have swept us away.

Praise be to the Lord, who has not let us be torn by their teeth. We have escaped like a bird out of the fowler's snare; the snare has been broken, and we have escaped.
Our help is in the name of the Lord, the Maker of heaven and earth.

I feel old today, Lord, I look in the mirror at tired eyes. I look back at the crisis just past, feeling that there are no overcomers in life, only survivers. Yet You are beside me, captive to circumstances with me, teaching me to see things from a perspective I've never realized was possible. Someday, even my salty tears will glitter like diamonds against the royal purple of my suffering...and others may stand in awe wishing perhaps that they themselves had had a share in it.

The Lord Surrounds His People

*Those who trust in the Lord are like Mount Zion, which
cannot be shaken but endures forever.*

Those who trust in the Lord are like Mount Zion, which
cannot be shaken but endures forever.
As the mountains surround Jerusalem, so the Lord surrounds
his people both now and forevermore.

The scepter of the wicked will not remain over the land
allotted to the righteous, for then the righteous might use their
hands to do evil.

Do good, O Lord, to those who are good, to those who are
upright in heart.
But those who turn to crooked ways the Lord will banish with
the evildoers.
Peace be upon Israel.

*Yesterday I felt like saying, either God
doesn't exist or he just doesn't want to get
involved with me. But I didn't dare to
verbalize a crooked thought. Sometimes I
want to lay off the commitment bit and
enjoy the pleasures of life. It's then I notice
You there, as always, an unmoveable rock
in my life, weighing down my conscience,
producing endurance because there is no
alternative. To whom should I go? You have
the words of eternal life!*

We Are Filled With Joy

Those who sow in tears will reap with songs of joy.
He who goes out weeping, carrying seed to sow, will return
with songs of joy, carrying sheaves with him.

When the Lord brought back the captives to Zion, we were
like men who dreamed.
Our mouths were filled with laughter, our tongues with songs
of joy. Then it was said among the nations, "The Lord has
done great things for them."
The Lord has done great things for us, and we are filled with
joy.

Restore our fortunes, O Lord, like streams in the Negev.
Those who sow in tears will reap with songs of joy.
He who goes out weeping, carrying seed to sow, will return
with songs of joy, carrying sheaves with him.

Yesterday I worried about my tomorrow.
Today I am living it. And I must see it as the
pinnacle of my life. If I haven't anything to
say about what God has done in my life
today then my neighbor has every right to
disbelieve in Him. Lord, every moment You
give Yourself to me in maximum strength.
I'm beginning to learn, whether sowing or
reaping or waiting out the winter season, it
is Your moment, Your day, filled with
potential and promise.

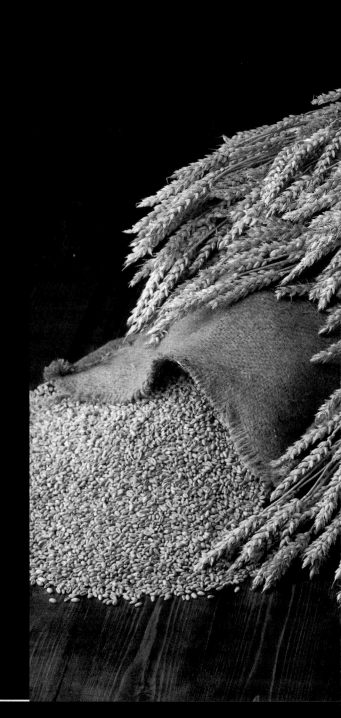

Children Are a Heritage

In vain you rise early and stay up late, toiling for food to eat— for he grants sleep to those he loves.

Unless the Lord builds the house, its builders labor in vain. Unless the Lord watches over the city, the watchmen stand guard in vain.
In vain you rise early and stay up late, toiling for food to eat— for he grants sleep to those he loves.

Sons are a heritage from the Lord, children a reward from him.
Like arrows in the hands of a warrior are sons born in one's youth.
Blessed is the man whose quiver is full of them. They will not be put to shame when they contend with their enemies in the gate.

Lord, these little "rewards" You've given me require more energy, more affection, more attention, more endurance than I ever dreamed of. But I have a feeling that one of the reasons you gave them to me is so that I might come to understand what reward really means. I assumed that having children and watching them grow would fill up the gaps in my own fulfillment. But you knew they would fill in the gaps of my maturity, helping me to grow, changing me gradually, narrowing my borders perhaps but enlarging my spirit, calling forth resources within me I never knew were there.

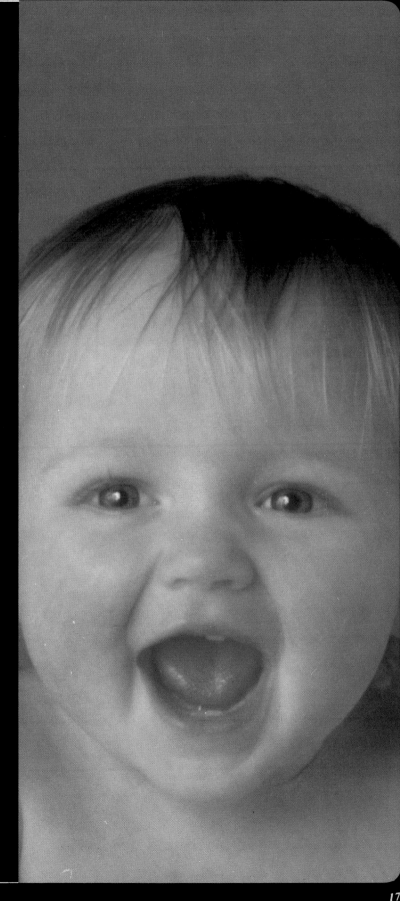

Like a Fruitful Vine

Your wife will be like a fruitful vine within your house; your sons will be like olive shoots around your table.

Blessed are all who fear the Lord, who walk in his ways.
You will eat the fruit of your labor; blessings and prosperity will be yours.
Your wife will be like a fruitful vine within your house; your sons will be like olive shoots around your table.
Thus is the man blessed who fears the Lord.

May the Lord bless you from Zion all the days of your life; may you see the prosperity of Jerusalem, and may you live to see your children's children.

Peace be upon Israel.

Early morning thumps deep down in the hollow of me give fresh reassurance of new life awaiting birth. I get wonder in my eyes like a child when I think about that special miracle living inside me now...tiny life like a bitty bud on a barren branch, holding all the potential of a whole world of spring. Lord, I am so glad. Others may not think we are prosperous, but soon our garden and our lives will bulge with the fruit of our labour and our love. What are empty status symbols compared to such moments of daybreak wrapped in happiness, morning light, and somebody else's arms?

But the Lord is Righteous

*May all who hate Zion be turned back in shame.
May they be like grass on the housetops, which withers before
it can grow; with it the reaper cannot fill his hands, nor the
one who gathers fill his arms.*

They have greatly oppressed me from my youth – let Israel
say – they have greatly oppressed me from my youth, but they
have not gained the victory over me.
Plowmen have plowed my back and made their furrows long.
But the Lord is righteous; he has cut me free from the cords of
the wicked.

May all who hate Zion be turned back in shame.
May they be like grass on the housetops, which withers before
it can grow; with it the reaper cannot fill his hands, nor the
one who gathers fill his arms.
May those who pass by not say, "The blessing of the Lord be
upon you; we bless you in the name of the Lord."

*When shadows fall across my corner of the
world and darken it, I am usually prepared
to endure them for a limited time. But faced
with the possibility of living with them
indefinitely, I start to lose courage, I begin
to complain. Still, it's life lived on your
terms, Father, that brings peace. So living
one day at a time I find it possible to go on,
until at last I learn what redemption is all
about.*

*I lift up my eyes
to You, to You whose throne
is in heaven.*

More Than Watchmen Wait for the Morning

I wait for the Lord, my soul waits, and in his word I put my hope.
My soul waits for the Lord more than watchmen wait for the morning, more than watchmen wait for the morning.

O Israel, put your hope in the Lord, for with the Lord is unfailing love and with him is full redemption.

Out of the depths I cry to you, O Lord; O Lord, hear my voice. Let your ears be attentive to my cry for mercy.

If you, O Lord, kept a record of sins, O Lord, who could stand?
But with you there is forgiveness; therefore you are feared.

I wait for the Lord, my soul waits, and in his word I put my hope.
My soul waits for the Lord more than watchmen wait for the morning, more than watchmen wait for the morning.

O Israel, put your hope in the Lord, for with the Lord is unfailing love and with him is full redemption.
He himself will redeem Israel from all their sins.

Impatient, pleading prayers get me nowhere. But there is the quiet, expectant prayer that makes my dreams come true. It comes to me in times of risking, when letting go of the past I grasp for things to come. It comes to me in assurance of Your forgiveness for mistakes, and in hope of the promises of Your Word.

Like a Weaned Child with its Mother

But I have stilled and quieted my soul; like a weaned child with its mother, like a weaned child is my soul within me.

My heart is not proud, O Lord, my eyes are not haughty; I do not concern myself with great matters or things too wonderful for me.
But I have stilled and quieted my soul; like a weaned child with its mother, like a weaned child is my soul within me.

O Israel, put your hope in the Lord both now and forevermore.

My attempts to stay on top of the endless details of daily living are so often futile. A little too much pressure here and there and I start to lose the peace You've given me. But I want to settle in against your shoulder, to slow down and live quietly within my limitations, and then to face the consequences calmly. I believe your sovereignty will never fail.

This is My Resting Place Forever and Ever

"One of your own descendants I will place on your throne– if your sons keep my covenant and the statutes I teach them, then their sons will sit on your throne for ever and ever."

O Lord, remember David and all the hardships he endured.

He swore an oath to the Lord and made a vow to the Mighty One of Jacob: "I will not enter my house or go to my bed-I will allow no sleep to my eyes, no slumber to my eyelids, till I find a place for the Lord, a dwelling for the Mighty One of Jacob."

We heard it in Ephrathah, we came upon it in the fields of Jaar:
"Let us go to his dwelling place; let us worship at his footstool– arise, O Lord, and come to your resting place, you and the ark of your might.
May your priests be clothed with righteousness; may your saints sing for joy."

For the sake of David your servant, do not reject your anointed one.

The Lord swore an oath to David, a sure oath that he will not revoke: "One of your own descendants I will place on your throne– if your sons keep my covenant and the statutes I teach them, then their sons will sit on your throne for ever and ever."
For the Lord has chosen Zion, he has desired it for his dwelling: "This is my resting place for ever and ever; here I will sit enthroned, for I have desired it– I will bless her with abundant provisions; her poor will I satisfy with food.
I will clothe her priests with salvation, and her saints will ever sing for joy.

"Here I will make a horn grow for David and set up a lamp for my anointed one.
I will clothe his enemies with shame, but the crown on his head will be resplendent."

Lord, you have chosen the place where You will rest, the place where You will reveal Your glory. It is in the center of Your people, the church. You will not rest until Your people are abundantly clothed, fed, and contented. Surely this is Your glory: that Your love and desire for Your people is pre-eminent to Your own rest, and an essential element in Your own identity.

When Brothers Live in Unity

How good and pleasant it is when brothers live together in unity!

How good and pleasant it is when brothers live together in unity!
It is like precious oil poured on the head, running down on the beard, running down on Aaron's beard, down upon the collar of his robes.
It is as if the dew of Hermon were falling on Mount Zion. For there the Lord bestows his blessing, even life forevermore.

My father tells how as a young soldier, he fell on an anonymous French battlefield to the sound of gunshot and shells exploding around him. Hours later and miles removed from that scene he woke up to the sound of laughing children; a sound so opposite to that of war that at first he thought he was in Heaven, and he has ever since associated this sound with the presence of God. If unity and peace are like precious oil and morning dew, symbols of God's annointing and blessing, then they are also like the innocent laughter of children, bouyant and renewing, given as a gift of grace when the hour is darkest.

Psalm 134

Minister by Night

Praise the Lord, all you servants of the Lord who minister by night in the house of the Lord.

Praise the Lord, all you servants of the Lord who minister by night in the house of the Lord.
Lift up your hands in the sanctuary and praise the Lord.

May the Lord, the Maker of heaven and earth, bless you from Zion.

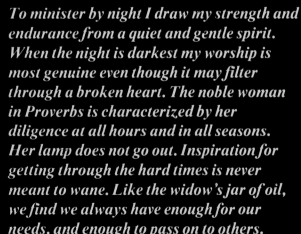

To minister by night I draw my strength and endurance from a quiet and gentle spirit. When the night is darkest my worship is most genuine even though it may filter through a broken heart. The noble woman in Proverbs is characterized by her diligence at all hours and in all seasons. Her lamp does not go out. Inspiration for getting through the hard times is never meant to wane. Like the widow's jar of oil, we find we always have enough for our needs, and enough to pass on to others.

His Treasured Possession

Praise the name of the Lord; Praise him, you servants of the Lord, you who minister in the house of the Lord, in the courts of the house of our God.

Praise the Lord, for the Lord is good; sing praise to his name, for that is pleasant.
For the Lord has chosen Jacob to be his own, Israel to be his treasured possession.

I know that the Lord is great, that our Lord is greater than all gods.
The Lord does whatever pleases him, in the heavens and on the earth, in the seas and all their depths.
He makes clouds rise from the ends of the earth; he sends lightning with the rain and brings out the wind from his storehouses.

He struck down the firstborn of Egypt, the firstborn of men and animals.
He sent his signs and wonders into your midst, O Egypt, against Pharaoh and all his servants.
He struck down many nations and killed mighty kings– Sihon king of the Amorites, Og king of Bashan and all the kings of Canaan– and he gave their land as an inheritance, an inheritance to his people Israel.

Your name, O Lord, endures forever, your renown, O Lord, through all generations.
For the Lord will vindicate his people and have compassion on his servants.

The idols of the nations are silver and gold, made by the hands of men.
They have mouths, but cannot speak, eyes, but they cannot see; they have ears, but cannot hear, nor is there breath in their mouths.
Those who make them will be like them, and so will all who trust in them.

O house of Israel, praise the Lord; O house of Aaron, praise the Lord; O house of Levi, praise the Lord; you who fear him, praise the Lord.
Praise be to the Lord from Zion, to him who dwells in Jerusalem.

Lord, Your treasuries are exciting to me. Like a child, I want to see what secrets You've got tucked away. I want to wander about in Your huge storerooms with big eyes. Sometimes You give me a peek. Among the jewels I most admire are Your judgement and compassion. And if I trust in You and submit to You I will take on Your character little by little. I can myself become a storehouse of Your treasure!

Psalm 136

His Love Endures Forever

Give thanks to the Lord, for he is good.

His love endures forever.

Give thanks to the God of gods.

His love endures forever.

Give thanks to the Lord of lords:

His love endures forever.

to him who alone does great wonders,

His love endures forever.

who by his understanding made the heavens,

His love endures forever.

who spread out the earth upon the waters,

His love endures forever.

who made the great lights–

His love endures forever.

the sun to govern the day,

His love endures forever.

the moon and stars to govern the night;

His love endures forever.

to him who struck down the firstborn of Egypt

His love endures forever.

and brought Israel out from among them

His love endures forever.

People who do not know the Lord must find when they look up into the starry sky from a mountain top or watch the everchanging ocean from a rocky cliff that the scene is vaguely imcomplete. For not knowing the creator, they have no one to say "Thank You" to. The feeling of thankfulness is common to humanity; one of those charming details of creation like the dots on a ladybug and the freckles on a red-haired boy that make us what we are. When we give thanks we fulfill an elemental part of our nature. And to give thanks to our creator in an attitude of faith even when we do not feel like doing it is an even more refined quality of our nature, convincing us we are more than body and soul, we are spirit!

Those who
sow in tears will
reap with songs
of joy.

He Led His People

With a mighty hand and outstretched arm;
> *His love endures forever.*

to him who divided the Red Sea asunder
> *His love endures forever.*

and brought Israel through the midst of it,
> *His love endures forever.*

but swept Pharaoh and his army into the Red Sea;
> *His love endures forever.*

to him who led his people through the desert,
> *His love endures forever.*

who struck down great kings,
> *His love endures forever.*

and killed mighty kings–
> *His love endures forever.*

Sihon king of the Amorites
> *His love endures forever.*

and Og king of Bashan–
> *His love endures forever.*

and gave their land as an inheritance,
> *His love endures forever.*

an inheritance to his servant Israel;
> *His love endures forever.*

to the One who remembered us in our low estate
> *His love endures forever.*

and freed us from our enemies,
> *His love endures forever.*

and who gives food to every creature.
> *His love endures forever.*

Give thanks to the God of heaven.
> *His love endures forever.*

History hasn't stopped teaching and instructing us in Your way. It points us toward Your purposes with people and nations, and points us to our responsibility. It points us not always to the right answers but to the right questions...questions that will prepare us ultimately to receive of Your power for establishing Your kingdom on earth.

How Can We Sing in a Foreign Land?

By the rivers of Babylon we sat and wept when we remembered Zion.
There on the poplars we hung our harps, for there our captors asked us for songs, our tormentors demanded songs of joy; they said, "Sing us one of the songs of Zion!"

By the rivers of Babylon we sat and wept when we remembered Zion.
There on the poplars we hung our harps, for there our captors asked us for songs, our tormentors demanded songs of joy; they said, "Sing us one of the songs of Zion!"

How can we sing the songs of the Lord while in a foreign land?
If I forget you, O Jerusalem, may my right hand forget its skill.
May my tongue cling to the roof of my mouth if I do not remember you, if I do not consider Jerusalem my highest joy.

Remember, O Lord, what the Edomites did on the day Jerusalem fell. "Tear it down," they cried, "tear it down to its foundations!"

O Daughter of Babylon, doomed to destruction, happy is he who repays you for what you have done to us– he who seizes your infants and dashes them against the rocks.

I can clearly visualize the mournful sobbing of the captives of Babylon. Tormented by painful memories and their own helplessness, in a swaying nostalgic dance they hang their harps upon the willows. They sit down by the banks of the river in their tattered rags, eyes glistening with tears, breasts heaving with longing for home. I feel the same, Lord, in my exile on earth. Misplaced and misunderstood I gaze toward the homeland not fully understanding the restlessness I feel. Then I realize I am not merely a foreigner in a strange land, prepared to stay awhile and settle for the comforts here. But I am a stranger in a foreign land, just passing through, on the move in my spirit. That's why my heart finds no rest.

The Lord Will Fulfill His Purpose

Though the Lord is on high, he looks upon the lowly, but the proud he knows from afar.
Though I walk in the midst of trouble, you preserve my life; you stretch out your hand against the anger of my foes, with your right hand you save me.
The Lord will fulfill his purpose for me; your love, O Lord, endures forever– do not abandon the works of your hands.

I will praise you, O Lord, with all my heart; before the "gods" I will sing your praise.
I will bow down toward your holy temple and will praise your name for your love and your faithfulness, for you have exalted above all things your name and your word.
When I called, you answered me; you made me bold and stout-hearted.

May all the kings of the earth praise you, O Lord, when they hear the words of your mouth.
May they sing of the ways of the Lord, for the glory of the Lord is great.

Though the Lord is on high, he looks upon the lowly, but the proud he knows from afar.
Though I walk in the midst of trouble, you preserve my life; you stretch out your hand against the anger of my foes, with your right hand you save me.
The Lord will fulfill his purpose for me; your love, O Lord, endures forever– do not abandon the works of your hands.

You have sometimes created, Father, special miracles just for me. You have shown me sometimes gently, sometimes explosively, Your favor. You have made yourself personal and intimate and reachable. As I walk further with You, I also experience Your dark and silent side. You become mysterious, distant, unknowable. It is in Your wisdom and mercy that You allow this as well. For You let me know that it is not my own whims, emotions, or even my needs that are in control. It is You who are in control. And I can trust You to finish what You've started in my spirit.

You Know Me, O Lord

O Lord, you have searched me and you know me.
You know when I sit and when I rise; you perceive my
thoughts from afar.
You discern my going out and my lying down; you are
familiar with all my ways.

O Lord, you have searched me and you know me.
You know when I sit and when I rise; you perceive my
thoughts from afar.
You discern my going out and my lying down; you are
familiar with all my ways.
Before a word is on my tongue you know it completely, O
Lord.
You hem me in–behind and before; you have laid your hand
upon me.
Such knowledge is too wonderful for me, too lofty for me to
attain.

Where can I go from your Spirit? Where can I flee from your
presence?
If I go up to the heavens, you are there; if I make my bed in the
depths, you are there.
If I rise on the wings of the dawn, if I settle on the far side of
the sea, even there your hand will guide me, your right hand
will hold me fast.

If I say, "Surely the darkness will hide me and the light
become night around me," even the darkness will not be dark
to you; the night will shine like the day, for darkness is as light
to you.

You have laid Your hand upon me Lord. I
can never go back to what or to where I was
before. I may struggle under your grip or I
may nestle closely into You. But life can
never be without the dimension of Your
presence again. You have laid Your hand
upon me, sometimes heavily, sometimes
caressingly, but the security of having it
there is something I never want to be
without.

How Precious Are Your Thoughts

I praise you because I am fearfully and wonderfully made;
your works are wonderful, I know that full well.

For you created my inmost being; you knit me together in my
mother's womb.
I praise you because I am fearfully and wonderfully made;
your works are wonderful, I know that full well.
My frame was not hidden from you when I was made in the
secret place. When I was woven together in the depths of the
earth, your eyes saw my unformed body. All the days
ordained for me were written in your book before one of them
came to be.

How precious to me are your thoughts, O God! How vast is
the sum of them!
Were I to count them, they would outnumber the grains of
sand.
When I awake, I am still with you.

If only you would slay the wicked, O God! Away from me,
you bloodthirsty men!
They speak of you with evil intent; your adversaries misuse
your name.
Do I not hate those who hate you, O Lord, and abhor those
who rise up against you?
I have nothing but hatred for them; I count them my enemies.

Search me, O God, and know my heart; test me and know my
anxious thoughts.
See if there is any offensive way in me, and lead me in the way
everlasting.

When I am in doubt of my abilities,
discouraged about my inadequacies,
confused about my identity I read Your
beautiful Word, full of promises and
perspectives that illuminate my potential
like the silver lining of the darkest cloud.

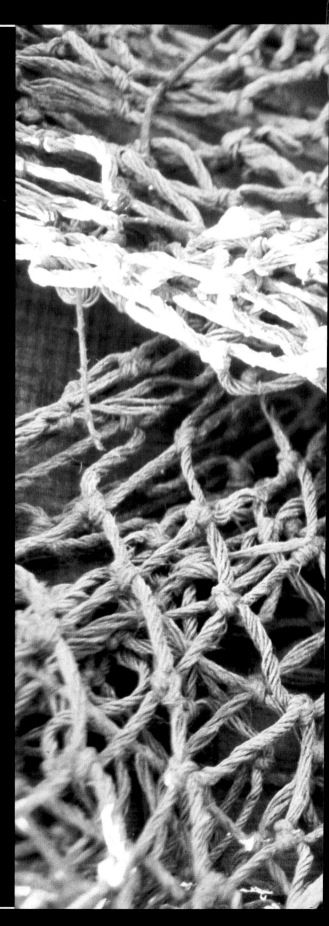

Psalm 140

The Lord Secures Justice

O Lord, I say to you, "You are my God." Hear, O Lord, my cry for mercy.
O Sovereign Lord, my strong deliverer, who shields my head in the day of battle– do not grant the wicked their desires, O Lord; do not let their plans succeed, or they will become proud. Selah

Rescue me, O Lord, from evil men; protect me from men of violence, who devise evil plans in their hearts and stir up war every day.
They make their tongues as sharp as a serpent's; the poison of vipers is on their lips. *Selah*

Keep me, O Lord, from the hands of the wicked; protect me from men of violence who plan to trip my feet.
Proud men have hidden a snare for me; they have spread out the cords of their net and have set traps for me along my path. *Selah*

O Lord, I say to you, "You are my God." Hear, O Lord, my cry for mercy.
O Sovereign Lord, my strong deliverer, who shields my head in the day of battle– do not grant the wicked their desires, O Lord; do not let their plans succeed, or they will become proud. *Selah*
Let the heads of those who surround me be covered with the trouble their lips have caused.
Let burning coals fall upon them; may they be thrown into the fire, into miry pits, never to rise.
Let slanderers not be established in the land; may disaster hunt down men of violence.

I know that the Lord secures justice for the poor and upholds the cause of the needy.
Surely the righteous will praise your name and the upright will live before you.

The innocent cannot always escape being hurt or misused. Oh Lord, trauma like that tends to make us bitter and hard when we ourselves must endure it. Yet we know by the example of Jesus, it is possible to gracefully bend with the blows. Your Word tells us there are pearls of grace in suffering, that even our deepest agonies are redemptive. We will wait. We pray for our persecutors and believe that You are for us, maintaining our cause in and through the humiliations of our life.

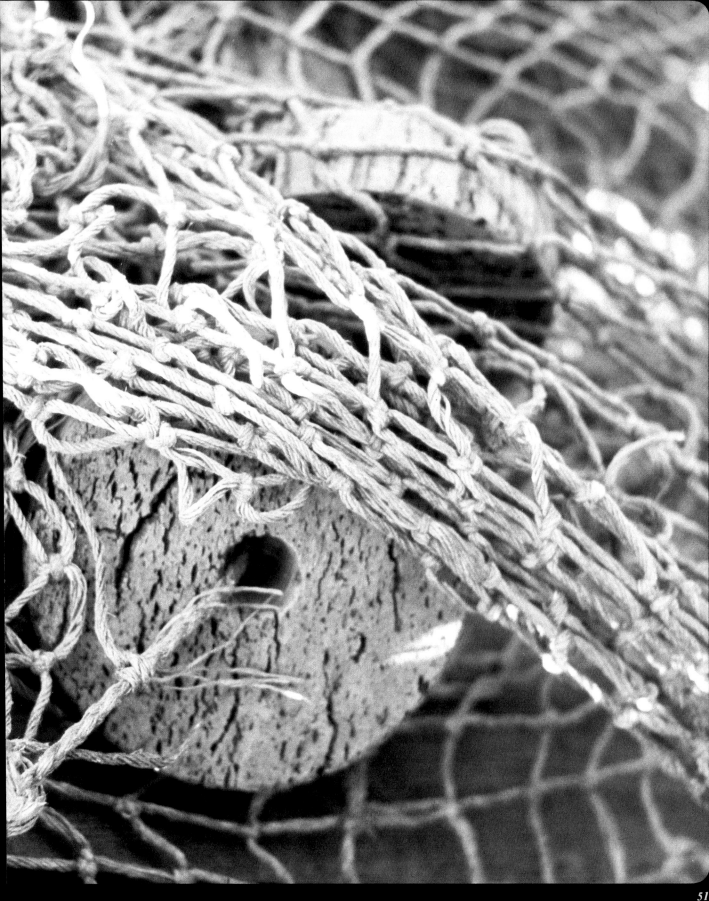

Come Quickly to Me

Let a righteous man strike me–it is a kindness; let him rebuke me–it is oil on my head. My head will not refuse it.

O Lord, I call to you; come quickly to me. Hear my voice when I call to you.
May my prayer be set before you like incense; may the lifting up of my hands be like the evening sacrifice.

Set a guard over my mouth, O Lord; keep watch over the door of my lips.
Let not my heart be drawn to what is evil, to take part in wicked deeds with men who are evildoers; let me not eat of their delicacies.

Let a righteous man strike me–it is a kindness; let him rebuke me–it is oil on my head. My head will not refuse it.

Yet my prayer is ever against the deeds of evildoers; their rulers will be thrown down from the cliffs, and the wicked will learn that my words were well spoken.
They will say, "As one plows and breaks up the earth, so our bones have been scattered at the mouth of the grave."

But my eyes are fixed on you, O Sovereign Lord; in you I take refuge–do not give me over to death.
Keep me from the snares they have laid for me, from the traps set by evildoers.
Let the wicked fall into their own nets, while I pass by in safety.

Lord, when I am burning with eagerness to serve You, why do I sense hesitation from Your side? Why do the visions You've given me take so long to materialize? I feel as if You've put me on a shelf, ignored and useless. Is it because the fruit of Your vine needs to mellow? You pour the clear liquid from bottle to bottle, allowing the sediment to settle, and then You lay it on its side to age. You baptise in fire and the Holy Ghost. But the longterm quality is developed in the cellar, unseen and unnoticed.

How precious to me are Your thoughts, O God! How vast is the sum of them! Were I to count them, they would outnumber the grains of sand.

I Tell the Lord My Trouble

I cry to you, O Lord; I say, "You are my refuge, my portion in the land of the living."
Listen to my cry; for I am in desperate need; rescue me from those who pursue me, for they are too strong for me.

I cry aloud to the Lord; I lift up my voice to the Lord for mercy.
I pour out my complaint before him; before him I tell my trouble.

When my spirit grows faint within me, it is you who know my way. In the path where I walk men have hidden a snare for me.
Look to my right and see; no one is concerned for me. I have no refuge; no one cares for my life.

I cry to you, O Lord; I say, "You are my refuge, my portion in the land of the living."
Listen to my cry; for I am in desperate need; rescue me from those who pursue me, for they are too strong for me.
Set me free from my prison, that I may praise your name.

Then the righteous will gather about me because of your goodness to me.

You don't spare me the problems and pain.
You just promise to make my possibilities
match their intensity. You stretch my faith
taut and give me no other alternative than
to trust in You.

I Hide Myself in You

Let the morning bring me word of your unfailing love, for I have put my trust in you. Show me the way I should go, for to you I lift up my soul.
O Lord, hear my prayer, listen to my cry for mercy; in your faithfulness and righteousness come to my relief.
Do not bring your servant into judgment, for no one living is righteous before you.

The enemy pursues me, he crushes me to the ground; he makes me dwell in darkness like those long dead.
So my spirit grows faint within me; my heart within me is dismayed.

I remember the days of long ago; I meditate on all your works and consider what your hands have done.
I spread out my hands to you; my soul thirsts for you like a parched land. *Selah*

Answer me quickly, O Lord; my spirit faints with longing. Do not hide your face from me or I will be like those who go down to the pit.
Let the morning bring me word of your unfailing love, for I have put my trust in you. Show me the way I should go, for to you I lift up my soul.
Rescue me from my enemies, O Lord, for I hide myself in you. Teach me to do your will, for you are my God; may your good Spirit lead me on level ground.

For your name's sake, O Lord, preserve my life; in your righteousness, bring me out of trouble.
In your unfailing love, silence my enemies; destroy all my foes, for I am your servant.

After a nightmare, I wake up feeling relieved that it was only a dream! But when the dreams of day fall apart and my visions start to die, I go to sleep feeling lonely and heavy hearted. I need to be assured of Your love in the darkness. Let the morning bring me this assurance. Your love may be all I've got now but it is enough. Someday You may ressurrect my dreams and restore my vision as well.

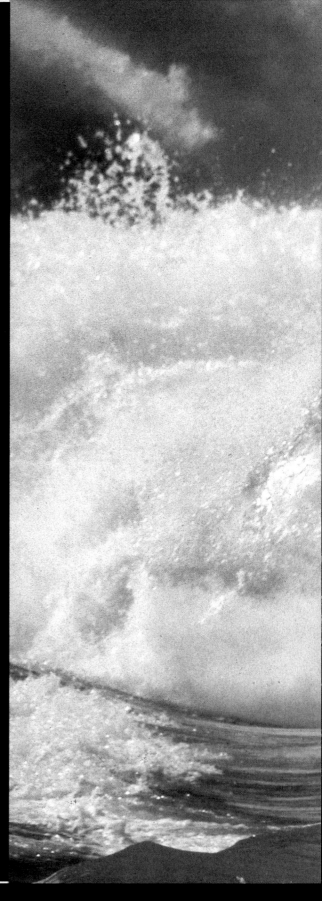

Blessed Are the Lord's People

Praise be to the Lord, my Rock, who trains my hands for war, my fingers for battle.
He is my loving God and my fortress, my stronghold and my deliverer, my shield, in whom I take refuge, who subdues peoples under me.

O Lord, what is man that you care for him, the son of man that you think of him?
Man is like a breath; his days are like a fleeting shadow.
Part your heavens, O Lord, and come down; touch the mountains, so that they smoke.
Send forth lightning and scatter the enemies; shoot your arrows and rout them.
Reach down your hand from on high; deliver me and rescue me from the mighty waters, from the hands of foreigners whose mouths are full of lies, whose right hands are deceitful.

I will sing a new song to you, O God; on the ten-stringed lyre I will make music to you, to the One who gives victory to kings, who delivers his servant David from the deadly sword.

Deliver me and rescue me from the hands of foreigners whose mouths are full of lies, whose right hands are deceitful.

Then our sons in their youth will be like well-nurtured plants, and our daughters will be like pillars carved to adorn a palace. Our barns will be filled with every kind of provision. Our sheep will increase by thousands, by tens of thousands in our fields; our oxen will draw heavy loads. There will be no breaching of walls, no going into captivity, no cry of distress in our streets.

Blessed are the people of whom this is true; blessed are the people whose God is the Lord.

My little three year old runs along the beach, scuffling with the waves, lost in her amusement. Fearing a sudden wave may take her unawares I watch her constantly. She is nothing more than a tiny red dot on an insignificant shore of all the shores of the world, but to me the most important thing in the universe. What I experience, Father, must be only a remnant of how You feel for your children. You are ready to part the heavens and show Your power in our defense, ready to rescue from the mighty waves.

They Will Celebrate Your Goodness

The Lord is good to all; he has compassion on all he has made.
All you have made will praise you, O Lord; your saints will extol you.
They will tell of the glory of your kingdom and speak of your might, so that all men may know of your mighty acts and the glorious splendor of your kingdom.

I will exalt you, my God the King; I will praise your name for ever and ever.
Every day I will praise you and extol your name for ever and ever.

Great is the Lord and most worthy of praise; his greatness no one can fathom.
One generation will commend your works to another; they will tell of your mighty acts.
They will speak of the glorious splendor of your majesty, and I will meditate on your wonderful works.
They will tell of the power of your awesome works, and I will proclaim your great deeds.
They will celebrate your abundant goodness and joyfully sing of your righteousness.

The Lord is gracious and compassionate, slow to anger and rich in love.
The Lord is good to all; he has compassion on all he has made.
All you have made will praise you, O Lord; your saints will extol you.
They will tell of the glory of your kingdom and speak of your might, so that all men may know of your mighty acts and the glorious splendor of your kingdom.

Father of Goodness, You originated the whole idea of being good. But we tend to moralize it and make it a victorian relic. We put it on our mantelpiece to admire as a charming curio, happy we needn't bother with it these days. But if we are made in Your image, our lives will not be fulfilling without being good. Your own abundant, creative example toward us nurtures the desire to be good and draws us toward you and toward others in repentence and restoration.

You Open Your Hand

*The Lord upholds all those who fall and lifts up all who are
bowed down.*
*The eyes of all look to you, and you give them their food at the
proper time.*
*You open your hand and satisfy the desires of every living
thing.*

*The Lord is righteous in all his ways and loving toward all he
has made.*

Your kingdom is an everlasting kingdom, and your dominion
endures through all generations.

The Lord is faithful to all his promises and loving toward all
he has made.
The Lord upholds all those who fall and lifts up all who are
bowed down.
The eyes of all look to you, and you give them their food at the
proper time.
You open your hand and satisfy the desires of every living
thing.

The Lord is righteous in all his ways and loving toward all he
has made.
The Lord is near to all who call on him, to all who call on him
in truth.
He fulfills the desires of those who fear him; he hears their cry
and saves them.
The Lord watches over all who love him, but all the wicked he
will destroy.

My mouth will speak in praise of the Lord. Let every creature
praise his holy name for ever and ever.

*Lord, You are like a patient, gentle mother
to your toddling children. And anyone who
has ever tried to be patient and gentle to
even a couple of toddlers knows how
difficult that can be. But you seem to thrive
on being interrupted by the cries from our
falls, our bruised egos, our fears. You
respond when we are hungry and thirsty,
and like two year olds we look to You
constantly, and follow you around. We start
out depending on you, learning to love you.
Eventually we will give back some of that
time and glory we stole away.*

He Upholds the Cause of the Oppressed

Blessed is he whose help is the God of Jacob, whose hope is in the Lord his God, the Maker of heaven and earth, the sea, and everything in them– the Lord, who remains faithful forever. He upholds the cause of the oppressed and gives food to the hungry.

Praise the Lord.

Praise the Lord, O my soul.
I will praise the Lord all my life; I will sing praise to my God as long as I live.

Do not put your trust in princes, in mortal men, who cannot save.
When their spirit departs, they return to the ground; on that very day their plans come to nothing.

Blessed is he whose help is the God of Jacob, whose hope is in the Lord his God, the Maker of heaven and earth, the sea, and everything in them– the Lord, who remains faithful forever. He upholds the cause of the oppressed and gives food to the hungry. The Lord sets prisoners free, the Lord gives sight to the blind, the Lord lifts up those who are bowed down, the Lord loves the righteous.
The Lord watches over the alien and sustains the fatherless and the widow, but he frustrates the ways of the wicked.

The Lord reigns forever, your God, O Zion, for all generations.

Praise the Lord.

God of love, you always have special concern for vulnerable people. Widows, orphans, prisoners, physically handicapped and strangers are among those for whom you make special provision. I am one of those people, feeling on the outskirts of society, easily wounded, bearing scars of trauma. Still, I can lift my head with hope. For I am learning daily to rely on You and the presence of Your Holy Spirit rather than in people alone. I am discovering the richness of a reigning Lord.

He Grants Peace to Your Borders

Praise the Lord. How good it is to sing praises to our God, how pleasant and fitting to praise him!

The Lord builds up Jerusalem; he gathers the exiles of Israel. He heals the brokenhearted and binds up their wounds.

He determines the number of the stars and calls them each by name.
Great is our Lord and mighty in power; his understanding has no limit.
The Lord sustains the humble but casts the wicked to the ground.

Sing to the Lord with thanksgiving; make music to our God on the harp.
He covers the sky with clouds; he supplies the earth with rain and makes grass grow on the hills.
He provides food for the cattle and for the young ravens when they call.

His pleasure is not in the strength of the horse, nor his delight in the legs of a man; the Lord delights in those who fear him, who put their hope in his unfailing love.

Extol the Lord, O Jerusalem; praise your God, O Zion, for he strengthens the bars of your gates and blesses your people within you.
He grants peace to your borders and satisfies you with the finest of wheat.

He sends his command to the earth; his word runs swiftly.
He spreads the snow like wool and scatters the frost like ashes.
He hurls down his hail like pebbles. Who can withstand his icy blast?
He sends his word and melts them; he stirs up his breezes, and the waters flow.

He has revealed his word to Jacob, his laws and decrees to Israel.
He has done this for no other nation; they do not know his laws.

It is You Lord, who bring down the wicked from his high horse. I don't have to try and do my share. Today I realized that when I responded so coldly and harshly to the ones who had wronged me, it was my way of coping under pressure and of taking revenge against a cold system. Besides being unkind and selfish, I only reinforce that system. But Your ways are unique. Your favor is with those who fear You and wait.

The eyes of all look
to You, and You give them their food
at the proper time. You open Your hand and
satisfy the desires of every
living thing.

The People Close to His Heart Praise Him

Praise him, all his angels, praise him, all his heavenly hosts.
Praise him, sun and moon, praise him, all you shining stars.
Praise him, you highest heavens and you waters above the
skies.

Praise the Lord.

Praise the Lord from the heavens, praise him in the heights
above.
Praise him, all his angels, praise him, all his heavenly hosts.
Praise him, sun and moon, praise him, all you shining stars.
Praise him, you highest heavens and you waters above the
skies.
Let them praise the name of the Lord, for he commanded and
they were created.
He set them in place for ever and ever; he gave a decree that
will never pass away.

Praise the Lord from the earth, you great sea creatures and all
ocean depths, lightning and hail, snow and clouds, stormy
winds that do his bidding, you mountains and all hills, fruit
trees and all cedars, wild animals and all cattle, small
creatures and flying birds, kings of the earth and all nations,
you princes and all rulers on earth, young men and maidens,
old men and children.

Let them praise the name of the Lord, for his name alone is
exalted; his splendor is above the earth and the heavens.
He has raised up for his people a horn, the praise of all his
saints, of Israel, the people close to his heart.

Praise the Lord.

Praise creates freedom and security. Praise
kindles the silent, struggling, less developed
sides of the personality. It actually helps
create the expression of the invisible quality
we seek. We can learn to look below the
surface and praise the unseen things we
believe are there, as well as the things we
see. Children thrive on praise, and God
actually abides in the praises of His people.

The Glory of All His Saints

Let Israel rejoice in their Maker; let the people of Zion be glad in their King.
Let them praise his name with dancing and make music to him with tambourine and harp.
For the Lord takes delight in his people; he crowns the humble with salvation.

Praise the Lord.

Sing to the Lord a new song, his praise in the assembly of the saints.

Let Israel rejoice in their Maker; let the people of Zion be glad in their King.
Let them praise his name with dancing and make music to him with tambourine and harp.
For the Lord takes delight in his people; he crowns the humble with salvation.
Let the saints rejoice in this honor and sing for joy on their beds.

May the praise of God be in their mouths and a double-edged sword in their hands, to inflict vengeance on the nations and punishment on the peoples, to bind their kings with fetters, their nobles with shackles of iron, to carry out the sentence written against them. This is the glory of all his saints.

Praise the Lord.

Lord, You knew that praise would enhance the praiser just as it does the one who is praised. You gave us the gift of praise to lift our spirits and motivate our actions. Freeing us of inhibitions, it is the mutual song of Bride and Bridegroom in the wedding chamber. You gave praise a dynamic quality so that when coupled with Your piercing Word, it can beautify the afflictions of the saints and it can storm the gates of Hell.

Let Everything Praise the Lord

Praise him with the sounding of the trumpet, praise him with the harp and lyre, praise him with tambourine and dancing, praise him with the strings and flute, praise him with the clash of cymbals, praise him with resounding cymbals.

Praise the Lord.

Praise God in his sanctuary; praise him in his mighty heavens.
Praise him for his acts of power; praise him for his surpassing greatness.
Praise him with the sounding of the trumpet, praise him with the harp and lyre, praise him with tambourine and dancing, praise him with the strings and flute, praise him with the clash of cymbals, praise him with resounding cymbals.

Let everything that has breath praise the Lord.

Praise the Lord.

Heaven will most likely be a noisy place. One of the most unique things that the writer of Revelations had to say about Heaven was that there was silence there for an entire half-an-hour! If eternal life already begins here on earth, perhaps we need to get into practice and use all the resources at hand to praise the Lord!

O Lord, what is man that
You care for him, the son of man that
You think of him? Man is like a breath; his
days are like a fleeting shadow.

*Give thanks to the Lord
for He is good. Give thanks to
the God of gods. Give thanks
to the Lord of lords.*